COPING WITH BEREAVEMENT

A practical guide to getting through grief

Written by Hugues Prion Pansius
Translated by Rebecca Neal

Health and Wellbeing   50MINUTES.com

COPING WITH BEREAVEMENT

- **Problem:** we will all lose a loved one at some point in our lives, and this experience is very painful and difficult to deal with. Whether sudden or not, the absence of a loved one disrupts our day-to-day activities and upsets the balance of our lives. Learning to live with this constant empty space can then seem impossible. How can you respect your grief while still moving forward to rediscover your taste for life? How can you survive bereavement without sinking into despair?
- **Aim:** to understand and overcome your grief.
- **FAQs:**
    - Is grief work necessary?
    - How long does grief last for?
    - Is it normal to cry all the time?
    - Will the pain go away more quickly if I ignore it?
    - I am smiling again and I have new plans. Should I feel guilty?

Although death comes to us all, it is still a taboo subject in Western society and the idea of it terrifies us. Even hearing it mentioned makes us uncomfortable. What, then, can we say about the death of a loved one, which for many people is a traumatic experience and can seem impossible to move on from? How can we survive the immense pain caused by the loss of a parent, partner, child or friend? Inevitably, all of us have lived through, are currently living through or will live through this difficult experience at some point and will spend a long, painful period mourning. The different phases of grief, including shock, anger, denial, guilt and depression, stir up a whole host of emotions, which are undeniably painful but which are nonetheless necessary if we are to accept the harsh reality.

> "I was 24 when my mother died of cancer. It was a huge shock for me and I felt as though I had fallen into a bottomless pit. For a long time, I felt disconnected from reality: nothing mattered to me any more and my life seemed to have no meaning. I was completely numb. Rather than accepting this unbearable reality, I tried to run from it and lived in a fool's paradise. I started to get better the day a wise person told me that my mother had never left me and that she was living in me." (Christian, 45)

In 50 minutes, you will understand the mechanisms that start working after bereavement, the practical side of these mechanisms, the importance of being supported by those around you, and some personal approaches you can take to help you in your journey towards acceptance. Finally, you will learn to identify the positive attitudes to adopt and the clichés to avoid when you want to support a loved one who is going through grief or explain death to a child.

WHAT IS BEREAVEMENT?

AN INTENSE AND UNIVERSAL PAIN

Bereavement, which comes from the Old English *bereafian*, meaning "to deprive of, take away by violence, seize, rob", refers to the period of distress and sadness following the death of a loved one. For us to be bereaved, we must have had a particular attachment to the person who has passed away. Otherwise, we would constantly be bereaved! The psychiatrist and psychotherapist Christophe Fauré also specifies that the intensity of bereavement is not determined by blood ties, but by how attached we were to the person. He further explains that bereavement can sometimes become a problem (although this is rare), for example if the bereaved person has a history of depression or if they had a conflictual relationship with the dead person. In this last case, they may develop a profound feeling of guilt, as they may feel that they unconsciously wished the person's death on them.

FREUD AND GRIEF WORK

In his 1917 essay "Mourning and Melancholia", Sigmund Freud became the first person to develop the concept of grief work. He claimed that this expression results from the loss of a loved one, and also from the loss of an object we are attached to. Grief work can therefore be defined as a long intrapsychic process resulting from the loss of an object a person is attached to. Through

While bereavement affects us all irrespective of gender, age or ethnicity, each culture has its own rituals and ways of dealing with the death of a loved one. For example, while the expression of grief is accepted and even encouraged in Western and African culture, it is viewed less positively in Asian and Muslim culture. In Asian society, emotions are expected to be kept private, while Muslims believe that containing grief shows that a person has accepted God's decision. As well as funeral rites and the expression of grief, each religion has very specific mourning periods and a different approach to funerals. For Buddhists, who believe in reincarnation, mourning lasts for 49 days, and at the end of this period a prayer is recited to help the dead person to be reincarnated. In Hinduism, the family of the dead person must lead a moderate lifestyle (no meat, alcohol, jewellery or make-up) during the mourning period, which lasts for 13 days and ends with a ceremony organised at the home of the dead person. The mourning period for Muslims is 40 days, during which the friends and family of the dead person must behave and dress soberly. At the end of this period, prayers are recited to help the dead person to ascend to heaven. In Judaism, there are five phases of mourning: *Aninut*, the period between death and the funeral; *Avelut*, the first seven days after the burial; *Sheloshim*, the first 30 days after the burial; *Yud Bet Chodesh*, the first 12 months following the burial; and *Yahrzeit*, the anniversary of the death.

SIGNIFICANT ADMINISTRATIVE TASKS

When you are stricken by grief following the death of a loved one, your life will be made even more difficult by a number of administrative and financial formalities, which will stop you from beginning your grief work. Although these tasks allow some people to take their minds off the pain they are feeling, for others they can become a burden that is too heavy to bear. Do not be afraid to ask the people around you for help if you do not feel strong enough to deal with these tasks.

During our lifetimes, we take out various insurance policies; we have bank accounts; we are registered with a healthcare provider and with the local authorities; we pay service providers every month, and so on. When we die, our family must notify all these people and organisations in order to stop these services and close our accounts. While some tasks can be carried out several weeks after the death, others must be done immediately.

To help you, here is a list of administrative formalities, in order of priority:

- **Register the death.** Unless your loved one died in a hospital or an official establishment (care home, prison, psychiatric institution), you must call a doctor to legally register the death of your loved one, so that you can declare it to the local authorities.
- **Contact a funeral home.** This company will take care of organising the funeral service, and will also declare the death to the local authorities, which must be done within five days.
- **Contact the banks.** If the deceased had accounts or a safe-deposit box at a bank, you should contact the bank as soon as possible in order to temporarily freeze them. This will suspend any current direct debits or standing orders.
- **Inform their employer or organisations in charge of paying benefits.** This will allow you to request the money owed (last instalment of salary, pension, holiday bonus, unemployment benefit, and so on) and avoid having to pay back incorrectly transferred money.
- **Cancel all important contracts.** Initially, focus on insurance contracts (home insurance, car insurance, health insurance, fire insurance, and so on) and contracts with service providers (water company, energy provider, internet and phone company, and so on). Inform them of the death. Depending on the contract, it may be cancelled or modified.
- **Inform the landlord or tenants of the deceased.** If your loved one was a landlord, you will need to inform their

tenants and give them the name of the person who will now collect their rent. If they were a tenant and did not live alone, you can contact the owner to determine how to proceed with the lease.

- **Value the estate of the deceased person.** This will allow you to determine whether Inheritance Tax will need to be paid on their estate and fill in the necessary forms to process this. You will need to calculate the total value of the person's assets (as well as "gifts", meaning any assets they gave away before they died) and debts in order to determine how much their estate is worth.

THE FIVE STAGES OF GRIEF

Although every bereavement is unique and each person deals with the pain caused by the loss of their loved one in their own way, it seems that the general process is relatively common to everyone. In the 1970s, the psychiatrist and psychologist Elisabeth Kübler-Ross theorised the stages that a bereaved person goes through. Kübler-Ross, who is known for her work in the field of palliative care, distinguished and described five distinct stages which we all go through during grief, and which allow us to express our emotions and accept the heartbreak of death. However, since every death and its impact on those left behind are different and cannot be compared to other situations, these stages are not fixed. As a result, an individual will not necessary experience all of these stages, or follow them in this order.

Finally, whether or not we know that the death of a loved one is imminent and can prepare ourselves for it, grief work is always necessary. Helen's account provides a clear illustration of this:

> "I knew that my father had virtually no chance of pulling through. He had lung cancer, and the doctors said that there was not much hope. I tried to prepare myself as well as I could, but the day he died was a huge shock. It was extremely painful. My visits to the hospital, which helped me because they still gave me a tiny glimmer of hope, stopped abruptly. Finding his room empty, then seeing him in his coffin, was a horribly painful and traumatic experience. In the end, all my preparation before his death was no help. It was only after his death that I had to start my grief work with the help of my loved ones." (Helen, 38)

Shock and denial

Finding out that a loved one has died generally leads to an initial phase of shock. We are left numb and dazed by this new reality, which we struggle to accept. Of course, we know that death is inevitable, but we cannot help railing against the injustice of it all and asking ourselves why him, why her, why now? This is followed by a phase of denial, which is a way for the bereaved person to defend themselves against a reality that they refuse to accept. During this phase, they are likely to constantly repeat things like "I can't believe it, it's impossible", "I'm going to wake up" and "this can't be happening".

After this phase of denial, which can last for very different periods of time depending on the individual and the circumstances surrounding the death, the bereaved person will inevitably realise that their loved one is not coming back. Once we have accepted this harsh reality, an intense and sometimes destructive wave of emotions washes over us like a tsunami.

Anger

Anger, which is sometimes completely irrational and often accompanied by a feeling of indignation, is an essential phase in the healing process. For the grieving person, it involves externalising the intense emotions they feel, but also finding a guilty party. Anger, which is driven by a feeling of injustice and intensified by the unpredictability and suddenness of death, can be directed towards the bereaved person themselves, the deceased person, a third party, or even a supernatural entity:

- against the bereaved person themselves: "I should have made him get help with his drinking";
- against the deceased person: "if she had taken care of herself, she would still be alive";
- against a third party: "the doctor diagnosed his cancer too late";
- against an imaginary or supernatural entity: "why does God let these things happen?", "why is Fate so cruel?"

The more the deceased person was loved, the stronger the feeling of anger is. However, according to Kübler-Ross, the more intense the anger is, the quicker it dissipates. It is therefore best to express it freely without trying to repress it.

Bargaining

Bargaining is a transition stage that allows us to come to terms with our pain. We are frustrated and have not yet accepted reality, so we try to bargain with this loss, for example by trying to imagine the different scenarios that could have prevented the inevitable outcome. We find ourselves saying "if only..." and questioning ourselves about our own guilt ("if I'd done this or that, maybe she would still be here!"). We also try to imagine what we could do to bring the person back.

> "Two months after I broke up with my boyfriend, he died in a car accident. It's strange, but for a long time I felt guilty and thought obsessively about his death. It was as if he died because we had broken up, as it had hit him hard. I told myself that if I hadn't broken up with him, he might still be alive." (Claudia, 33)

If we are dealing with our own impending death, bargaining manifests itself in phrases expressing despair and attempts at negotiation ("let me have one more Christmas with my children", "if I could just have a few more years...", "I promise to change if I survive", and so on), and, in some cases, in a return to spirituality ("God, I will do whatever you want if you just let me live", "I will go to church every day if I have to, but let me get better", and so on).

This phase ends when our rational mind brings us back to reality: the person we have lost is never coming back.

Depression

Once we have accepted the reality of death, sadness, which is now more intense than ever, and the impression that the pain will never fade overwhelm us. Furthermore, the consequences of this loss start to be felt (financial and administrative difficulties, family conflicts, and so on). Depression sets in, bringing a whole host of symptoms with it: a loss of interest in everyday activities; intense, constant tiredness; appetite loss; trouble concentrating; mood swings; etc. This is the phase where we withdraw into ourselves and become isolated, because everything now seems meaningless. Its duration varies widely from one person to another, but it can last for several months or even several years, as was the case for Eric. It is therefore essential to be able to count on the unwavering support of the people around you.

> "When my brother died, my life was turned upside down. We were very close, and we also ran a small business together. After he died, I couldn't enjoy anything, I hardly went out any more, and I sold the company. When my loved ones asked me about it, I pretended that I was fine and just needed a change. It wasn't until I lost a lot of weight that they really started to worry. Then, it hit me that I couldn't keep going like this. I spoke to my GP about it, and he referred me to a psychiatrist. I think it took me at least a year to break free of my depression. It was a long, tedious task, but I feel so much better now." (Eric, 51)

This stage, which is very important in the grieving process, is entirely normal. However, if your depression does not get better and seriously disrupts the balance of your daily life, or has major consequences (losing your job, worsening physical or mental health, complete social isolation, and so on), you may need to see a specialist.

Acceptance

In theory, acceptance is the final stage of grief work. We finally understand and accept that the deceased person is gone for good. However, this does not mean that we have forgotten them or that we no longer feel any sadness, but we are now able to talk about our loved one without falling apart, and although the pain is still there, it is bearable. Acceptance also marks the start of the rebuilding phase. We are now ready to learn how to live with this permanent absence and we are once again able to enjoy life's little pleasures.

Prince William's confession

Prince William has spoken on several occasions about his grief following the death of his mother, Princess Diana, who died in a car accident on 31 August 1997. He said that the days immediately following bereavement are marked by "a sense of profound shock and disbelief that this could ever happen to you", adding that "real grief does not hit home until much later", accompanied by the regret of no longer being able to talk to and love the deceased person. He also said "Never being able to say the word 'Mummy' again in your life sounds like a small thing. However, for many, including me, it's now really just a word – hollow and evoking only memories" (*The Telegraph*, 2009).

HOW CAN YOU OVERCOME BEREAVEMENT AND START LIVING AGAIN?

HAVE YOU MOVED PAST YOUR BEREAVEMENT?

Sometimes, a few weeks or a few months after losing a loved one, we feel as though we are doing better and have managed to mourn and turn the page. However, this improvement could be an illusion, as you may still be stuck in the denial or bargaining phase. Some everyday behaviours or particular factors may alert you and make you aware that you may not quite have reached the end of this long process.

TEST: HAVE YOU OVERCOME YOUR BEREAVEMENT?

- You no longer want to see your friends and family, and going out at all demands a superhuman effort.
- You think that your life is meaningless and you no longer make any plans for the future.
- You burst into tears for no reason or at the slightest irritation.
- All your thoughts are focused on the death of your loved one, to the point that it is the only thing you think about.
- Your memories with the deceased person haunt you and make you sad.
- You suffer from insomnia and have recurring nightmares.

- You constantly feel mentally and physically tired.
- You struggle to focus on your work or everyday tasks.
- You have lost an unusual amount of weight.
- You have completely lost your libido.

If at least three of these ten statements apply to you, your grief work is not finished yet. Talk to the people around you about it, evaluate the stage you are at, and adopt some day-to-day habits to help you to overcome your pain.

TEN TIPS FOR GETTING THROUGH YOUR BEREAVEMENT

Give yourself the time you need. There is no fixed length for mourning. Everyone experiences it differently depending on their personality and the relationship they had with the deceased person. Do not feel guilty if you move past your bereavement quickly: this does not mean that you did not love the person or that you are insensitive. On the other hand, do not beat yourself up if you do not seem to have reached the end of the process after several months. You must give yourself the time you need to accept the death and express the emotions you are feeling. It is only when you feel calm and ready that you will be able to create a new bond with the deceased person and reinvest in your life.

Accept pain and face up to your loss. Trying to ignore your grief by throwing yourself into work, denial, alcohol or drugs is not the answer. All this will do is temporarily numb your mind and stave off your pain, which will come back with a vengeance afterwards. Accept the fact that you have lost someone you love, that this has hurt you deeply, and that you feel lost, empty and devastated. These emotions are natural and healthy, and you have the right to feel them, even if modern society tends to be uncomfortable with displays of emotion. Face up to reality and tell yourself: "I have lost someone who I loved a lot and I am in pain. I am really suffering." By saying this and talking about the emotions it inspires in you out loud, you are giving yourself permission to experience your bereavement without feeling guilty.

Express your feelings. Let your suffering out instead of repressing it. Scream, cry, throw things on the floor, punch a pillow, and so on, but above all, do not keep your pain inside. Whether you share your emotions with your loved ones or put them on paper through writing or drawing, expressing them helps you to free yourself from them more quickly and prevents negative tension from building up in your body, which could lead to complications later on.

Spend time with your friends and family. The people around you are probably the most vital source of support in your grief work, since in most cases your loved ones knew or had met the deceased person. This makes it easier to express your pain and the loss you are feeling, but also to remember the good times you shared and the stories about the person's life. Exchanging memories will allow you to evoke their memory tenderly and calmly, because if you are sad, it means that the deceased person had a positive impact on your life. Why not focus on that and remember all the times, laughter, jokes, hugs and experiences you shared?

Mourn their death, but at the same time, celebrate their life.

Do not try to forget your loved one. Getting rid of everything that reminds you of the deceased person (clothes, photographs, personal items, and so on) will not help you to overcome your grief. Accept that they were a part of your life, that they had an impact on your it and that they are important to you. If you try to escape your unbearable suffering by denying their existence and their death, you are not respecting their memory. However, it is also important not to go too far in the opposite direction. Turning the deceased person's bedroom into a shrine that nobody is allowed to touch will not help you any more than erasing every trace of their time on earth. You need to find the right balance. Make up a box of memories containing photographs, a personal object you are attached to, a letter from them and a perfume that reminds you of them, and keep it in a wardrobe.

Take care of yourself. During the depressive stage of grief work, it is not uncommon for people to neglect their lifestyle and completely let themselves go. However, taking care of yourself is essential if you want to overcome your pain. Prepare tasty, healthy meals, go for a walk in the woods or a park to remind yourself of life's little pleasures, do some exercise as an outlet for your emotions (especially anger), keep to a good sleep schedule, watch a funny or relaxing film depending on how you feel, and so on.

Turn your suffering into a ritual. According to the psychiatrist Christophe Fauré, both religious and nonreligious rites of passage among men stem from "the need to reconcile psychological pain and an existential quest when a member of their community has just died"[1] (2012). As well as the funeral service, which happens shortly after the death, rituals such as visiting their grave, taking part in memorial events or praying may help you to manage your bereavement better on a day-to-day basis. If you feel the need, you can go regularly to the cemetery to reflect or talk to your loved one; if you are religious, you can go see a priest, imam or rabbi to share your pain and say a few prayers.

Join a support group. If you are in too much pain and do not know where to turn, there are many peer support groups or associations that let you share your feelings with other people in the same situation. These groups work based on the principles of echoes and resonance: each participant talks about their experiences, which will inevitably resonate with someone else, resulting in a sort of bond and understanding between the members of the group. Depending on the type of bereavement you are going through, some organisations are more specific: loss of a child, support after a suicide, support after a long illness, support for the loved ones of murder victims, and so on. As well as psychological help, these support groups can also give you legal and administrative advice to help you to manage the practical aspects linked to the death.

Consult a specialist. If support groups and peer support services do not appeal to you, or if they have not helped you and you feel that you are losing control, do not hesitate to seek help from a healthcare professional. Consult your

---

1. This quotation has been translated by 50Minutes.com.

GP, who will be able to recommend medication if you are suffering from severe depression, or refer you to a therapist.

Pay tribute to the deceased person. When your pain lessens, or at least becomes bearable, and your bereavement is coming to an end, it may be appropriate and helpful to pay tribute to the deceased person on key dates, such as their birthday, your wedding anniversary, the day you met or another significant date. This may be an opportunity to get together as a family or as friends and remember the good times you had with the deceased person. Far from being morbid, these gatherings will let you share memories and happiness.

TEARS CAN MAKE YOU FEEL BETTER

In the modern world, tears are sometimes seen as a sign of weakness, and we tend to hold them back out of embarrassment or shame. However, they have the power to free us from our pain, so let them flow. Sooner or later, you will cry less and a profound feeling of relief will wash over you. According to Dr Alexander Lowen, crying lets us avoid the harmful spiral of anxiety and depression. The psychologist Judith Orloff says that crying encourages the body to release endorphins, the hormone linked to wellbeing, which are also released when we exercise (Lorenzo, 2015).

HOW CAN YOU HELP A LOVED ONE DEAL WITH BEREAVEMENT?

THE RIGHT ATTITUDES TO ADOPT

It is not always easy to find the right words to comfort a bereaved person. Faced with their pain, we often feel at a loss. Bereavement is such an intimate and emotional situation that it is difficult for us to understand exactly what the other person is feeling, even if we are empathetic towards them. However, being there and listening without judging are often enough to help.

Be there

This seems to go without saying, even if, paradoxically, we often think that people who are suffering want to be alone. While they have a lot of people around them in the early days and are swept up in the whirlwind of administrative work linked to the death and the organisation of the funeral, your grieving loved ones need to have support and people around them during the calm after the storm more than anything else. It is at this point that they find themselves face to face with the void in their life left by the deceased person. Generally, this means the weeks following the funeral. They can soon find themselves isolated and helpless as they try to deal with their pain, which is still raw. You must therefore be there for them over the long term. Without being intrusive, suggest going out somewhere, pay them a visit at home or simply call them. The important thing is that they feel they can count on you if they need to.

Listen

> "Talking about our pain is the first step in consoling oursel-
> ves."[2] (Albert Camus, 1913-1960)

Simply being there is not enough: you must also genuinely listen without judging. Let your loved one put their suffering into words rather than showering them with unhelpful, insensitive advice like "forget about it" or "think about something else". You must also be able to listen to their silences, which are just as important as the time they spend speaking, and encourage others around them to do the same. It is essential that the bereaved person feel supported by all their loved ones rather than by just one person, who may not be psychologically strong enough to deal with the situation over the medium and long term.

Talk openly about the deceased person

We wrongly think that it is better to avoid talking about the deceased person in front of those who are grieving, since talking about them will cause them more pain, so we try our best to avoid all conversations on this topic. Although this attitude is normal and understandable, it does not help in the slightest. Keep in mind that all your loved one's thoughts are focused on the cause of their grief; it is therefore highly likely that they feel the need to talk about the deceased person, especially if you knew them well. Furthermore, this approach often proves liberating, as it stops them from burying or even denying reality and instead allows them to

---

2. This quotation has been translated by 50Minutes.com.

confront it head on. In this way, they will gradually come to terms with the fact that the person they love is no longer there. You should therefore avoid leaving things unsaid and talk openly about the subject. In any case, if they really do not want to talk about it, they will tell you.

Learn how to identify the different emotions caused by bereavement

Be aware of the different stages a bereaved person goes through, because being there, listening and respecting their pain necessarily implies trying to understand the emotions they are dealing with. Consequently, do not be surprised if they suddenly get angry and start accusing everyone of playing a part in their loved one's death. During the depression phase, it is not unusual for the bereaved person to isolate themselves and avoid certain people. For example, a parent who has lost a child may avoid couples with children because they dread the unbearable sight of this picture of happiness, which now belongs to the past. They may be angry, sad or embarrassed, and your role is to concentrate on these different emotions, to listen to them without criticising and, possibly, to question them with the person in distress.

> "I was expecting my first child, and my husband and I were very excited. Unfortunately, I had a miscarriage. I was devastated and struggled to deal with the reactions of the people around me, who said that I should not be in such a state because it was still just a foetus at that stage, that I would have another one, and so on. Of course, I knew that the situation must be more difficult for parents who had lost a 10-year-old child, but I still felt immense pain. One of my friends gave

birth a few weeks after my miscarriage and I couldn't bring myself to go congratulate her at the hospital. She was very understanding and never held it against me. I have since given birth to my first child and been able to overcome my pain, even though I still sometimes think about this little person who was just waiting to be born." (Valentine, 32)

Do not compare your experiences of bereavement

Although it is helpful to pay attention to similarities in the way of dealing with the loss of a loved one, you should not compare your grief with that of others, since everyone responds to this painful period differently. Do not criticise a loved one because they seem more affected by the loss of their grandfather than you were when you lost your mother. Besides blood ties between individuals, emotional bonds, the nature of the relationship and even each person's degree of sensitivity play a role in dealing with the loss of a loved one. As such, although you should feel free to share your own experience of bereavement to show your loved one that they are not alone in their struggle, avoiding making comparisons and saying things that could complicate their grief work, even if they seem trivial to you.

Avoid platitudes and clichés

It is normal and human to feel lost when dealing with a lo-ved one's pain and to be tempted to rely on commonplaces and platitudes. Avoid this trap! Although it is customary to use set phrases like "my condolences" at the funeral, it is better to avoid come clichés such as "85 is a good age to die, she lived a good life!" and "Don't be sad, he's watching over you now". Although some people may find comfort in them, others will resent you for your lack of tact and empathy. The fact that someone's mother was 85 when she died does not make the pain any less intense. As such, rather than speaking in platitudes that will do more harm than good, think about the following Sufi proverb: "if the thing that you are going to say is less beautiful than silence, do not say it"[3]. Think before you speak, and be satisfied with being there and listening if you cannot find the words to comfort your loved one.

SUPPORTING A CHILD IN THEIR GRIEF WORK

Bereavement is painful at any age, but our way of dealing with this experience varies depending on our psychological and emotional maturity. Children can also lose a loved one, and react differently from adults because they do not always have a concrete understanding of the concept of death. Very young children do not realise that they have just lost a loved one; however, they are like sponges and absorb all the emotions of the people around them, which can lead to anxiety. When they are a little bit older (usually around four), they start to become aware of death, but they do not yet fully grasp that it is irreversible. Consequently, they will not express their sadness because they are under the impression that the situation is only temporary and their loved one will come back soon. After the age of six, the child becomes fully aware of death and of the suffering and despair that it brings, and in some cases may feel guilty that

---

3. This quotation has been translated by 50Minutes.com.

they could not do anything to stop this painful loss. When an adolescent is facing the loss of a loved one, they may feel particularly strong emotions, as this period already entails major hormonal imbalances that affect their mood and outlook on the world.

To support your child in their grief work, it is important not to hide the truth from them out of a desire to protect them, because they also need to grieve.

To help them to do so, it is important to:

- spend time with them and reassure them;
- avoid taking them away from their friends and family;
- let them ask as many questions as they want and give them simple, accurate and honest answers;
- let them attend the funeral, provided they are old enough;
- give them the opportunity to keep the memory of the deceased person alive by visiting their grave if they ask to, or carrying out activities in remembrance of them.

If you feel unable to explain or support your child in this phase, feel free to go to a bookshop or library. There are a range of books that explain the notion of death using simple, age-appropriate language.

HOW CAN YOU GET BACK ON TRACK AFTER MOURNING?

If you think that you have come out the other side of this mourning period and fully accepted the loss of your loved one, and feel ready to make new plans in your life, now is the time to rebuild your social life and reopen yourself to the world in order to avoid falling back into depression.

- **Take care of yourself:** treat yourself to an outdoor getaway, exercise, eat a healthy, balanced diet, and make sure you get enough sleep.
- **Throw yourself back into your social life:** meet new people, go out for a drink with friends or plan a weekend away with them, and get reacquainted with a friend you have lost touch with.
- **Make plans for the future:** plan a trip, open yourself up to the possibility of a relationship, and so on.

Of course, rediscovering your taste for life does not mean forgetting the deceased person; you will think about them from time to time and evoke their memory with tenderness and love, but above all you will be aware that nothing should stop you from living, because life is a gift. Indeed, people who have experienced this kind of trauma often begin to look at life differently. They become better at putting life's events into perspective by taking a step back and making the most of the present.

This newfound awareness should be seen as a blessing, because it can help us to develop a calmer, less selfish and

more externally focused philosophy of life. Often, the stress
of modern life prevents us from taking ten minutes a day to
wonder at the world. Starting today, we can take the time to
contemplate the beauty of the world and make the most of
other people, who will not be around forever.

FAQS

IS GRIEF WORK NECESSARY?

Yes, because it allows you to move on from the suffering and listlessness you may find yourself experiencing after a death. The loss of a loved one results in a separation from the world around you. When grief work is carried out, without rushing and while still respecting your grief, it can help you to reconnect with life.

HOW LONG DOES GRIEF LAST FOR?

It is difficult to say, because the length of the bereavement period varies from one individual to another, and depends on a very wide range of factors, including the intensity of the relationship with the deceased person and the violence of their death. Everyone should grieve at their own pace. Grief work cannot be shortened: there is no way of speeding it up or skipping steps. We can consider that grieving is over once the wound has healed and the pain is no longer unbearable: this is a sign that reality has been accepted. However, the end of the mourning period does not mean that any pain stemming from the loss of a person will never return. Even though you will still feel pangs of sadness from time to time, they will gradually become less acute.

IS IT NORMAL TO CRY ALL THE TIME?

Crying is a completely normal way of externalising suffering. It releases endorphins, which can help us to let go of our anxieties. It is therefore not recommended to try and hold back your tears. Over time, you will inevitably cry less often. On the other hand, some people do not cry, but this does not mean that they are not sad.

WILL THE PAIN GO AWAY MORE QUICKLY IF I IGNORE IT?

Trying to run away from reality by ignoring it will not help you, because denial never solves anything. It is completely misguided to think that concealing the source of your suffering will make you feel better. Acknowledge your pain and accept all the emotions you are experiencing, from anger to despair, even if you feel like you are losing control. If you bury your feelings and ignore your pain, it will catch up with you sooner or later.

I AM SMILING AGAIN AND I HAVE NEW PLANS. SHOULD I FEEL GUILTY?

Absolutely not! This is the whole aim of grief work. Smiling again means that you have accepted reality, that you are taking back control of your life and that you are able to appreciate everyday pleasures again. On no account does this mean that you have forgotten your loved one or that you have moved on to something else; you have simply given them a place that no longer stops you from living your life.

We want to hear from you!
Leave a comment on your online library
and share your favourite books on social media!

FURTHER READING

BIBLIOGRAPHY

- Bolleau, A. (2012) Vivre un deuil. *Doctissimo.fr.* [Online]. [Accessed 30 May 2017]. Available from: <http://www.doctissimo.fr/html/psychologie/bien_dans_sa_peau/ps_3188_deuil_article2.htm>
- Fauré, C. (2012) *Vivre le deuil au jour le jour.* Paris: Albin Michel.
- Kübler-Ross, E. and Kessler, D. (2005) *On Grief and Grieving: Finding the Meaning of Grief Through the Five Stages of Loss.* London: Simon & Schuster.
- Levert, I. (No date) L'épreuve du deuil. *La-psychologie.com.* [Online]. [Accessed 30 May 2017]. Available from: <http://www.la-psychologie.com/deuil.htm>
- Lorenzo, S. (2015) Pourquoi je pleure? Une question difficile sur laquelle la science n'a pas encore complètement tranché. *Huffingtonpost.fr.* [Online]. [Accessed 30 May 2017]. Available from: <http://www.huffingtonpost.fr/2015/11/17/pourquoi-je-pleurequestion-difficile_n_8580534.html>
- Mazelin-Salvi, F. (2010) Accepter le temps du deuil. *Psychologies.com.* [Online]. [Accessed 30 May 2017]. Available from: <http://www.psychologies.com/Moi/Epreuves/Deuil/Articles-et-Dossiers/Accepter-le-temps-du-deuil>
- Senk, P. (2011) Deuil : un processus naturel de cicatrisation naturelle psychique. *Sante.lefigaro.fr.* [Online]. [Accessed 30 May 2017]. Available from: <http://sante.lefigaro.fr/actualite/2011/11/03/15297-deuil-proces-

sus-naturel-cicatrisation-psychique>
- The Telegraph (2009) *Prince William speaks of shock at losing his mother, Princess Diana: full statement.* [Online]. [Accessed 30 May 2017]. Available from: <http://www. telegraph.co.uk/news/uknews/theroyalfamily/4983438/ Prince-William-speaks-of-shock-at-losing-his-mother-Princess-Diana-full-statement..html>
- Yick, A. and Gupta, R. (2002) Chinese cultural dimensions of death, dying, and bereavement: focus group findings. *Journal of Cultural Diversity*, pp. 32-42.

ADDITIONAL SOURCES

- Cobb, R. (2012) *Missing Mummy: A book about bereavement.* London: Macmillan Children's Books.
- Ginsburg, G. (2004) *Widow to Widow: Thoughtful, Practical Ideas for Rebuilding Your Life.* Cambridge, Massachusetts: Da Capo Press.
- Harper Neeld, E. (2006) *Seven Choices: Finding Daylight After Loss Shatters Your World.* Austin, Texas: Warner Books.
- Ironside, V. (1997) *'You'll Get Over It': The Rage of Bereavement.* London: Penguin.
- Levy, A. (2000) *The Orphaned Adult: Understanding and Coping with Grief and Change After the Death of Our Parents.* New York: Perseus Publishing.
- Lewis, C.S. (2013) *A Grief Observed.* New York: HarperCollins.
- Lukas, C. (2007) *Silent Grief: Living in the Wake of Suicide.* London: Jessica Kingsley Publishers.
- Samuel, J. (2017) *Grief Works: Stories of Life, Death and*

Surviving. London: Penguin.
- Stickney, D. (2004) *Water Bugs and Dragonflies: Explaining Death to Young Children*. Cleveland, Ohio: The Pilgrim Press.
- Tatelbaum, J. (1993) *Courage to Grieve: Creative Living, Recovery and Growth Through Grief*. London: Vermilion.

www.50minutes.com

Ebook EAN: 9782806299857

Paperback EAN: 9782806299864

Legal Deposit: D/2017/12603/403

Cover: © Primento

Digital conception by Primento, the digital partner of publishers.

Made in the USA
Monee, IL
07 July 2026